JIM BRYANS

PERFECTIONISM

**The Essential Guide On How to Overcome
Perfectionism, Learn The Effective Ways on How to Stop
Being a Perfectionist and Embrace Your Imperfections**

Descrierea CIP a Bibliotecii Naţionale a României
JIM BRYANS
   PERFECTIONISM. The Essential Guide On How to Overcome Perfectionism, Learn The Effective Ways on How to Stop Being a Perfectionist and Embrace Your Imperfections / Jim Bryans. – Bucharest: Editura My Ebook, 2020
   ISBN

JIM BRYANS

PERFECTIONISM

**The Essential Guide On How to Overcome
Perfectionism, Learn The Effective Ways on How to Stop
Being a Perfectionist and Embrace Your Imperfections**

My Ebook Publishing House
Bucharest, 2020

CONTENTS

CONTENTS

INTRODUCTION

Perfectionism is the belief that perfection can and should be attained. In an extreme form, perfectionism is a belief that work and products that are anything less than perfect are completely unacceptable. That later of which is actually what they call in psychology, a maladaptive belief, and often causes problems in day to day functioning. Many business owners in the world today can be described, and are often self-described, perfectionists.

The epidemiology for internet based business owners is not different. Perfectionism can be a driving force for success, but in the fast paced world internet businesses, it is truly a double-edged sword. It can serve to push forward the business, or it can serve to destroy it. The internet based business owner must learn how to weld this weapon well to succeed. The purpose of this article is to encourage all internet based business owners to avoid these maladaptive behaviors and to spend their time in taking action rather than thinking about it.

Internet based business owners spend countless hours putting together information products for consumers all over the world. These good range from E-books, and reports, to software and services. They are often required to produce a large amount of information and services in a short amount of time. A major hitch in this system arises when the business owner buys into the concept that all products and services must be perfect before released or before another service or product can be started.

If one would take a look at some of the most successful businesses in the world today, they would quickly see that this is not the way that they do business. Successful, money making businesses release their products before they are "perfect," because they know that the product will progress along the line towards perfection at a much quicker pace if consumers are involved in the process. Think of it this way, how many minds are better at perfecting a product, one or two, or one or two hundred? By overcoming this concept of perfectionism, internet based business owners can actually increase their profits and decrease their time commitment, while at the same time producing a better product.

The temptation for many internet based business owners is to try to get everything right on the first try. This simply defies logic for many reasons. The first of which is that it totally negates the major underlying learning theories. That is, people learn from repetition and from making mistakes. It's called the law of approximations. Products improve as the approach, or approximate perfection. Just as one rewards children for even the approximations of good behavior, so does the consumer reward the business owner when they approximate correctly.

Consumers are forgiving and want to be involved in the producing of a product that they will enjoy. It's call buy-in. Consumers buy-in to a product when they are allowed to provide feedback. When consumers feel apart of the process, that translates into profit for the business owner! That brings up the next reason; perfection is in the eye of the beholder. This will be examined more in detail in the preceding paragraphs, suffice it to say here that a producer can not know what a perfect product is until she has received feedback from the consumer.

The goal is this: to release products in a timely manner as to receive constant feedback from consumers. This will allow for the producer to then get a better picture of what the consumer thinks is perfect, and to adjust accordingly. If product hit the mainstream only seldom, there is little feedback that can then be put back into the production system. It is the old theory of priming the pump. One used to have to put a little water in the well pump to get it to pump out water in return.

The same principle works in the internet based information product world. It is ideal to release a product, get some feedback, rework the product and release again. Or even learn from the feedback received from one product to aid in the production of another product. Literally, the more perfect an internet based business owner tries to be with an initial product, the more likely it is not to be a perfect product.

The following paragraphs will serve to illuminate some of the common perfectionists traps that internet based business owners typically fall prey to. It is not always easy to recognize them, especially in oneself. But the following paragraphs seek to help one look inside himself to find the traps that maybe hindering success. They will also seek to give some alternatives and ways to deal with the perfectionist's traps.

THE COMMON TRAPS

The common traps that will be examined are: When being a perfectionist is bad; perfection is in the eye of the consumer; Momentum: The success maker; The quicksand of perfectionism; and A Win/Win situation. If one wants their internet business to thrive, he must avoid these traps at all cost. By avoiding them, the internet based business owner will not only become a better person, but also the owner of a more successful business!

Trap One: When Being a Perfectionist Is Bad

Often times being a perfectionist is thought about in positive terms. They do things right the first time and do not have to do them again. This might be a good mantra for carpenters (measure twice, cut once) and mechanics (who wants a mechanic who truly works solely on trial and error?), but it is not a great way to run an internet based business. There are four key ways in which being a perfectionist can prevent an internet based business owner from becoming successful: too much time is spent in planning and not action, little or no feedback is received from the consumers, success is not allowed to build upon success and perfection can be a relative term.

Planning is important. It is foolish to set out to build a home or a business or even a product without a plan. The problem arises when the plan becomes the purpose. The plan is not the purpose, the product, or the home or the business is the purpose. It is very much like the old adage that one can not see the forest because of the trees.

If a business owner gets to in depth and detailed in the planning process, focus is lost on the overall mission of providing a product that the consumer will enjoy. Too much time spent in the planning process can also deter from the taking action part of the process. The goal is to get the product out to the public; too much time spent on trying to make the product perfect will often irritate the public who is waiting for it, thus having the opposite effect that one would hope for.

Another fall back about being a perfectionist is that it often limits the amount of consumer feedback that is received. It can also taint the way in which such feedback is received by the owner as well. One can not stress enough how important it is to get feedback from the consumers to whom one is selling. Trying to produce a product without consumer feedback is like trying to hike through the Rockies without a map or compass. One is just going to end up lost, and possibly eaten by a bear. Consumer feedback is the compass that guides an owner to provided and later one producing a more perfect product. Tied along in this is that the more time one spends in perfecting a product, the more personal interest is put into it. That can be a good thing, but as often as not; it can also be a bad thing. Too much personal interest can cause constructive criticism and feedback to be rejected.

Success has to be allowed to breed success. Fear of failure has to be challenged and in the end overcome so that success can take it place. Once success has taken seed, then in continues to grow in and of itself. It is like the first time someone rides a roller coaster. They are often scared to death, but when the ride is over, they find new strength they never thought they had. The next ride might be a step- up and fear may still be sensed, but once the ride is over, new strength is found once again! This could go on ad infinitum. The point is that success snow balls, but it cannot get started if a product is not allowed to start rolling.

Being a perfectionist is bad when being perfect is relative. And in the world of internet-based businesses, it is. What might be a perfect product to an owner and her staff may not be a perfect product to the consumers. One has to take the chance and go out where the rubber meets the road to find out what perfect really is in their world. A product must be allowed to grow into perfection; much like a person goes through pain and effort to build muscles. How can one attain what one cannot define? And how can a business define perfect without letting the consumers be a part of the refining process? The obvious answers to these questions are in the negative. The goal of perfection may also be a maladaptive goal as well. Remember, the ultimate goal is to be successful, not to be perfect. And often times striving to perfection weighs one down in the journey to success.

All that to say that a business owner must learn to take a chance. Being a perfectionist may help in other arenas of life, but in the internet based business world, it can cripple a business. In other words, a perfectionist's attitude may very well suffocate success. That being said, once the ball gets rolling, once the perfectionists beliefs are laid aside, success has the room and air necessary to survive, grow and thrive.

Prior planning does prevent poor performance, but obsessive planning will result in no performance at all. It is not hard, but it requires the letting go of some maladaptive behaviors that are often well engrained. The results, however, will more than compensate for any displeasure in giving up perfectionism.

Trap Two: Perfection Is In the Eye of the Beholder

This trap has been eluded to several times already throughout the article, but now it will be developed more fully. The basic premise is that one does not know if a product is truly "perfect" until it is available on the market so that consumers can provide feedback. Once again, the idea is that perfection in regards to a product or service is extremely relative. Without releasing a product to the public, one is left in his uncertainty about how good or "perfect" the product is.

In actuality, a person can spend many more hours working on a product that would have already been considered "perfect" in the eyes of the consumers. Thus, time and money were wasted. An internet based business owner has no chance of getting ahead and ultimately becoming a success playing this "perfection" game. Do not despair: there is hope for the perfectionist! There are several basic mental process that one can go through to get the product out there without it having to be "perfect."

The first is that the business owner must lose the fear of failure. That does not mean they she has to be fearless. A person without fear is not successful, they are stupid. However, a person who learns to control her fears and move past them becomes a very successful and dangerous person in the world of internet based businesses. No one likes to be criticized or critiqued. Critiques are often taken as attacks on personal value and character. They are not. They are comments and suggestions about the product and have nothing to do with a person's intrinsic value. If they are taken as such, both the owner and the product are in major trouble. So, one must first learn to differentiate oneself and one's ideas from their value as a person. They are very different things and when this is realized, one begins to lose the fear of failure and the fear of peer evaluation.

Another mental process that can help one over the hump of releasing "imperfect" products and services is to simply think positive. There is a lot of power in positive thinking. Catastrophizing only causes more fear and anxiety. One must learn to look at her product in a positive light and have faith in their own abilities to produce a quality product. It is the negative thinking and judgmentalism that drives perfectionism.

By always seeing their product or service in a negative light, the perfectionist business owner will be extremely hesitant to release any product out for evaluation. These only lead down the spiral of imperfection and failure. By thinking positively about a product or service and having confidence in it, one is more likely to release it without wasting time fretting and worrying over it. It will also allow the public to provide more feedback and thus lead down the road to a better product and ultimately to success.

A third way to overcome the fear of letting a product out before it is "perfect" is to just do it. There is no way to know if a product is truly perfect until it is release and feedback from consumers is received.

Holding the product back and thinking, and rewriting, and redesigning only serve to put the product behind on its journey to "perfection."

The owner cannot know that is "perfect" without input from consumers. It is like looking into a foggy mirror. An internet based business owner may have an idea as to what the product should be or how it should look, but it is not until the consumer blows some fresh air onto the mirror that an owner can truly see how the product should be. This means that the owner must simply let go and put it on the market. Just do it. That is the best way to find out what a good product should look like.

There are many other ways to address this problem, and the important thing is that each business owner find what works for him or her.

Some can conquer their fear of failure and more ahead calmly, allowing the market to decide what a perfect product looks like. Other can use the power of positive thinking to adjust the way they view feedback and thus increase the likely hood of them releasing a product or service onto the market sooner. Others may need to just "suck it up" and "just do it." This can also be a very effective way of increasing productivity and eliminating the need for being "perfect".

The point is that one will never know if a product or service is perfect until the consumer tells them so! That cannot be found out with the product or service taking up space on some hard drive somewhere.

Have faith and take the first step out. One can not go forward without taking a step and one can not be successful without getting products out on the market. It is that simple. With a little positive thinking, some tough skin, and a just do it attitude, success is just around the corner.

Trap Three: Ending the Success Maker before It Stats: Momentum

This is one of the more damaging traps. It is also one that many business owners do not even realize that they have fallen into. This is the results factor. Without seeing results, one often times gets discouraged and spins their wheels, going no place. It is important, therefore, to keep a "don't get it right, just get it going" mentality.

This is the attitude that leads to the success maker of momentum.

The faster one sees results, the more motivated they are to do more, to improve, and to move ahead. Much like the self-perpetuating perfectionist spiral, the momentum spiral feeds off of itself. The more one produces and gets going and gets on the market, the more one is free to do more projects and so on and so forth. It is like a snow ball rolling down the mountain. It may start off like a snow cone, but it will end up like an avalanche.

Momentum in a business is built when a series of success are accumulated, one right after the other. For example, momentum in sales is built by closing rapid fire deals. For the internet based business owner, it might be built through producing quick growth and meeting a lot of short term goals quickly. This builds a great amount of confidence in oneself as well as the products or services that one is providing. Momentum in business equals motivation x productivity.

One can easily see how this equation can just build and build on itself. The more one is motivated, the more productive they typically are, therefore the constants grow and the outcome (momentum) grows exponentially. When momentum is experienced, one has a great sense of achievement that feeds into ones motivation to keep going. Here are some following tips to find some momentum and to keep it going.

The first tip is to formulate a vision and stick to it. This is basically a way to gauge progress and success. A good way to go about this is to form a mission statement with an implicit goal(s). Then simply list the steps that it will take to get from the current spot to where the mission statement leads. Be as explicit as possible. These steps can serve as milestones to measure progress a long the way. One thing to remember is that sometimes things do take time. Rome was not built in a day and neither will momentum. It will take several days of motivation and productivity to get a good rhythm of momentum going, but it will happen. Just be patient.

Another tip is to start off running. This will go against the grain of a perfectionist, but remember, out goal is not perfection, it is success. Successful people have momentum and momentum is built by gazelle like intensity. A gazelle never goes anywhere nonchalantly. They decide where they want to go and then get there without any hesitation With a firm vision and mission statement as guides, one can take off with gazelle like intensity. Once the balls gets rolling and gets rolling fast, it is extremely hard to slow it down or to stop it. That is what is called momentum.

This tip is a hard one for many people. To build momentum and to keep it going, one must break out of his comfort zone. Going full speed with gazelle like intensity out of one's comfort zone can be really scary. Things will be happening fast and doubts will start to arise. The key is to take them as they come. Recognize the doubts, acknowledge them, and then refocus on the guiding vision and mission statement.

Risks are often involved, but they must be taken. This is not condoning erratic and irresponsible behavior; rather it is supporting and encouraging strong, decisive behavior that is vision and mission driven.

Another tip is one that most people have heard over and over in their lives, but it especially applies to those in the internet based business world. One must learn to accentuate the positive and eliminate the negative. If the day starts out begrudgingly, there is a good chance that no momentum will be built that day. Even when times are hard and the economy is down, look for positives to build upon. Positive thinking begets more positive thinking. It can quickly become an epidemic and before one knows it, everyone they work with is thinking positively, which leads to more motivation and more productivity which leads to? That's correct, momentum!

Lastly, one must always keep one's goals and mission at the forefront of his mind. That will help when resistance or obstacles are encountered. There are many things that will try to throw one off track, such as the belief that perfectionism is the way to go in the business world. But a good look at ones mission and vision will serve to refocus and to harness motivation once again and put it into service. Momentum can and will carry a business a long way in the journey of success. It only takes a spark to get a wild fire burning, and it only takes a little motivation and some productivity to be well on one's way to having that great success maker: momentum.

Trap Four: The Quicksand of Perfectionism

The fourth trap is the quicksand of perfectionism. It looks safe, but it will eventually swallow a business whole. Perfectionists often get stuck while others are out making money. It is a really easy thing to do actually. It is very easy to get caught trying to balance too many things at once or even just trying to produce one "perfect" product or service.

The reason it is called quicksand is that perfectionism, by nature, will pull one down. But it will not do it immediately, it will do it slowly and sometimes even without the person realizing what is happening. That is the case more often than not. One person is stuck in the quicksand of perfectionism, and instead of trying to get out, they just look around and wonder why they are not succeeding like the others who are around them. Well, have no fear! The following are some sure fire survival skills that can help any internet based business navigate the jungle of the business world.

The first thing a business owner must do to avoid the quicksand of perfectionism is to know her surroundings. It can be very tempting to get caught up in looking and correcting every little detail in a product or service. Micro managing looks like a lot of fun. But what it does is take attention away from the overall picture and goal of success.

Yes, one needs to look before they step. No one wants to step onto a snake! But if one bends down to examine every little footstep, they will quickly loose track of where they are (as well as loosing momentum). It is important to know what worked in the past, and to have an idea of what might work in the future. That will give one a general picture of their business surroundings and can help to alleviate the need to be a perfectionist.

A second skill is to know how to swim. It is somewhat common knowledge that when one falls into quicksand, the more they struggle the harder it is to get out. Aimless fighting and struggling only serves to waste energy. Focused motions with purpose, such as swimming, however, are sure fire ways to escape quicksand. The same rings true in the business world.

If one is caught in micro managing and perfectionism, the best thing he can do is to look for solid ground and be focused about getting out. Panicking will only cause more problems. If one sees that their business is not succeeding, panicking will only cause more problems in the long run. The owner needs to calm down, focus on where they want to go, and start making small, purposeful movement to get there.

The third survival skill is to know when to ask for help. There is no shame in asking other competent people for advice or for a hand, particularly if one is drowning in the quicksand of perfectionism. No one should be too proud to ask for help. This also includes knowing one's limitations as well as strengths and weaknesses. There may also be others out there who have struggled with perfectionism and can assist in overcoming it. Perfectionism can and will choke out the success in a business. It is imperative to be able to navigate through the jungle of internet business, and often a guide who has been there before can be very helpful.

That last survival tip is to not give up. One might find himself in the middle of a bit vat of perfectionist quicksand. That last thing to do is to give up and sink it. That attitude of "That's just the way I am" will ultimately doom a business. That may be the way a person is now, but it is not they way that they must always be. People can change, and people do change everyday.

The key is to not give up and give in to one's own perfectionist tendencies. It will be challenging and one may find themselves stuck more than once while others are succeeding. But that is okay. The important thing is to keep at it, to keep the mission and vision in focus. They will be the guide to get one out of the quicksand and ultimately back on track to building momentum and success.

These four survival skills will help any internet based business owner navigate the jungle of their work and ultimately survive and escape the quicksand of perfectionism. By being aware of what has worked in the past and what is likely to work in the future, one can avoid the temptation of perfectionism all together. By knowing how to swim and being focused one can escape the quicksand of perfectionism if she gets caught it in.

By knowing when to ask for help one can avoid wasted timed trying to get out of the quicksand alone. And by not giving up and by having a never say die attitude, one ensures that they will quickly be on the road to success once again. These four tips could be the difference between great success and ultimate failure.

Trap Five: Avoiding the Win/Win Situation

The fifth trap is not so much something that someone gets herself into as much as what she avoids. Often times internet based business owners and entrepreneurs think that failing is a let down. In all actuality just the opposite is true. A "failure" is not a let down, it is a learning experience. Remember back at the beginning of the article when approximations were discussed. This is where they come in.

A "failure" is just when the market lets an entrepreneurs know how to change the product or service to be a better approximation of that which it desires. Even when an owner does not get it "right" there is almost always positive gain. They learn how to better accommodate the consumer the next time around. Knowledge is always helpful.

One often hears the adage, "If at first you don't succeed, try, try again." Well the consumer market is a self correcting organism. It communicates through successes and failures and anything in between. It is important to note here that success and failure is not a black and white issue. They are on a continuum, with success at one end and failure on the other.

There can be different degrees of success as well as different degrees of failure. And even a "complete" failure is not all bad. There are always lessons to be learned when one is faced with defeat. Take, for example, the history of the airplane. What if Orrville and Wilbur Wright had stopped at their first prototype because it did not fly? Honestly, all that would have happened was that someone else would be famous for the first airplane. They took their failures and used them to learn and adapt for the future. That's ultimately what all business owners and entrepreneurs must do as well.

As with all the other traps mentioned, there are some key ways to avoid this trap and to promote and nurture the win/win situation. The win/win situation is simple. Either one puts a product on the market and it is met with success, which is a win. Or, one puts a product out on the market and it's a "failure" but they receive lots of consumer feedback, which is also a win. Success or failure can be viewed as a win. And it hinges on a couple common concepts: acceptance and commitment.

Acceptance is the idea that there are things that one can not change. The fact that there will be both success and failures in one's business career is unchangeable. It must be accepted. It also includes the concept that it should not be judged. Having both failures and successes in business is neither good nor bad, it just is.

Every business owner or entrepreneur encounters them both at sometime. It is a given in the game that is being played, therefore it must be accepted. Once one accepts that he will face defeat and failure from time to time, he can focus on learning from those opportunities, instead of avoiding them. If life is lived solely for the purpose of avoiding failure, then life is truly not lived at all.

The second part is called commitment. This means that one will continue on the course, not matter what it encountered.

Facing obstacles and failures can be very daunting and scary. Many business owners quit after their first failure. If one accepts that both failures and successes will be met, then one can easily, fully commit to the journey itself. Failures are not longer let downs and deal breakers.

They are simply opportunities to learn and to have greater success in the future due to the experience. Commitment will ensure that one can experience the win/win situation. If one has a success, they are committed, if one has a failure, they are still just as committed as before.

It is this kind of business person, one who both accepts the nature of the game and commits to playing the game, that ends up successful and making money while other watch from the sidelines. The trap is the avoidance of failure; the skills to survive that trap are acceptance and commitment.

If one runs their business to avoid failure, then they will always face the lose/lose situation. Perfectionism sets in, along with fear and anxiety. Quicksand forms around their feet and they are easily swallowed up by it. By accepting failure, one by passes the need and temptation to be "perfect" all together and allows for his product to be shaped and molded by those who will purchase it, the consumers.

Learning is the key. All internet based business owners or entrepreneurs must become life long learners. The markets will change, technology will change, and even the rules of the business game will change. But if one remains committed to the journey, and accepts both the success and the failures, they have created an environment that will promote more and more success. Accept the failures as learning opportunities and commit to keep going whenever the path gets tough, and you will quickly find yourself on the road to success.

DEAD TO PERFECTIONISM,
ALIVE TO SUCCESS!

Being a perfectionist can be a good thing in many circumstances. Being a perfectionist and an internet based business owner, however, does not mix well. It can be like oil and water. To be a successful internet based business owner, one needs to be quick to take action. A perfectionist attitude and comportment work against that need.

Whether one is producing software, e-books or other internet based goods and services, it is important for him to be quick to act to be able to make money and be a success.

A strong temptation for all business owners around the world has been to get everything right on the first try. To put it bluntly, that is impossible. An internet based business owner must be both willing and able to release products in a timely manner as to receive feedback.

The feedback serves as a learning tool to more clearly see what a "perfect" product is. Holding on to a product until it is "perfect" in the owner's eyes is almost a sure fire way to insure that it will not be perfect.

There were five traps that business owners and entrepreneurs should avoid that have been discussed in this article. None of them are the answer to perfectionism problem. A danger with providing lists is that the perfectionist is tempted to try to keep the list perfectly. This article is not meant to be treated as such. The traps are simply guidelines and mental strategies to help business owners become more successful. They are not an end in and of themselves. They are a means to an end, and should be looked upon as such.

The first trap discussed how being a perfectionist can prevent internet based business owners from becoming successful. There were four key ways in which being a perfectionist can prevent an internet based business owner from becoming successful that were discussed: too much time is spent in planning and not action, little or no feedback is received from the consumers, success is not allowed to build upon success and perfection can be a relative term. Do not get caught up in the list. The purpose is to promote action. Action leads to success.

The second trap discussed the issue of how perfect is in the eye of the consumer. A business owner will never truly know if a product is "perfect" until it is available to the consumer. The consumer can then provide feedback on the product back to the owner. This feeds the production cycle and leads to better and better products. Better products lead to more business, and so on and so forth. But if the product or service never leaves the owner, the product or service can never truly improve.

The third trap discussed was the trap of stopping momentum. Taking action and avoiding being a perfectionist leads to productivity, which turns into momentum. Remember the formula; motivation x productivity equals momentum. And momentum leads to success.

Reaching goals quickly and seeing results help build up to this thing called momentum. And remember, momentum is not the end goal; success is the ultimate end goal. Momentum is simply one of the best ways to get there, but momentum cannot be started until action has been taken.

The fourth trap is the quicksand of perfectionism. Perfectionism will suck one down and ultimately leave one stuck in the sand while others around them are making money. It can be a frustrating thing to realize when one is stuck. Keep focused and stay on track. Learn to swim and learn when to ask others for help. The business world truly is a jungle, but it can be survived. And even more than that, it can be thrived in!

Those are your best bets on getting unstuck.

The last trap was when business owner avoid the win/win situation. A win/win situation is when a product is release in a timely manner.

Either the consumer will love it or they will provide feedback on how it can be improved. That is a win/win. Getting caught up in perfectionism creates a lose/lose situation that no one wants to be in.

When the day is done and when all the computers are turned off, the important thing to ask oneself is, "Did I accomplish my goals? Were my actions in line with my vision and my mission?" If they were not, then the next day needs to start out with some action taking. Success builds upon and breeds more success. Perfectionism can quickly choke out any momentum that leads to success, so it is important to know how to avoid the key traps of perfectionism.

Printed by Libri Plureos GmbH in Hamburg,
Germany